Dream Big ◆ Happy Reading

Andrea Coke

Molly Morningstar
Carnival Girl

Written by
Andrea Coke

Illustrated by
M. Fernanda Orozco

Copyright © 2021 Andrea Coke
All rights reserved. This book or parts thereof may not be reproduced in any form, stored in any retrieval system, or transmitted in any form by any means—electronic, mechanical, photocopy, recording, or otherwise—without prior written permission of the publisher.

ISBN: 978-1-7773883-9-3 (Paperback)
978-1-7773883-8-6 (Hardcover)
978-1-7778327-0-4 (Ebook)
978-1-7778327-1-1 (Activity Book)

Front cover image by M. Fernanda Orozco
Book design by Praise Saflor
Printed in Canada.
First printing edition 2021.

Toronto, ON, Canada
www.abcbooknook.com
Adventures In Reverie Publishing Corp.

To my father, who showed me the importance of being rooted in love, family, and culture.

This book belongs to:

_____

"Today is the day I've been waiting for!" shouts Molly Morningstar. I can't wait to go to the Kiddie Carnival Parade!"

Every year, Molly and her parents head to the city to celebrate the big Caribbean cultural festival. Dancing in the parade is Molly's favorite thing to do.

Molly carefully puts on her costume. For this special day, Molly chose the grandest, most sparkling, most gigantic outfit she could find. She carefully places the glittery crown on her head.

"These bright pink feathers add just the right touch," Molly says to her mom. "There's a prize for the best costume, and I plan to win."

As the entire family piles into the streetcar, Molly and Boomer sit in a row by themselves. Molly's costume is so big—and so grand—that there is no room for anyone else.

Soon the driver calls out,

"Kiddie Carnival Parade, next stop!"

"Oh no!"

Molly cries, as she steps down from the streetcar.

"I lost a feather! My costume is wrecked! How will I win?"

"Don't worry, it's just one silly feather," Papa says.

"You still have two feathers and your costume is still a showstopper, kiddo."

Molly and her parents weave past birds, fairies, and pirates.

"There they are!" Molly shrieks, as she sees her friend Emma chatting with other friends.

Molly gazes at the crowd. All of her friends and neighbors are here. Their masks and outfits are beautiful, but Molly is sure hers is the best.

Mama gives Molly a bear hug.
"Have fun, Molly Morningstar."

Papa gives her a little flag.
"Wave your flag,
Molly Morningstar."

The bandleader hands Molly a whistle. "Make some noise, Molly Morningstar."

Mama and Papa watch from the sidewalk as the parade begins.

Children prance and dance in the street. The musical sound of the steel drums floats in the air, reminding everyone of the beautiful Caribbean islands.

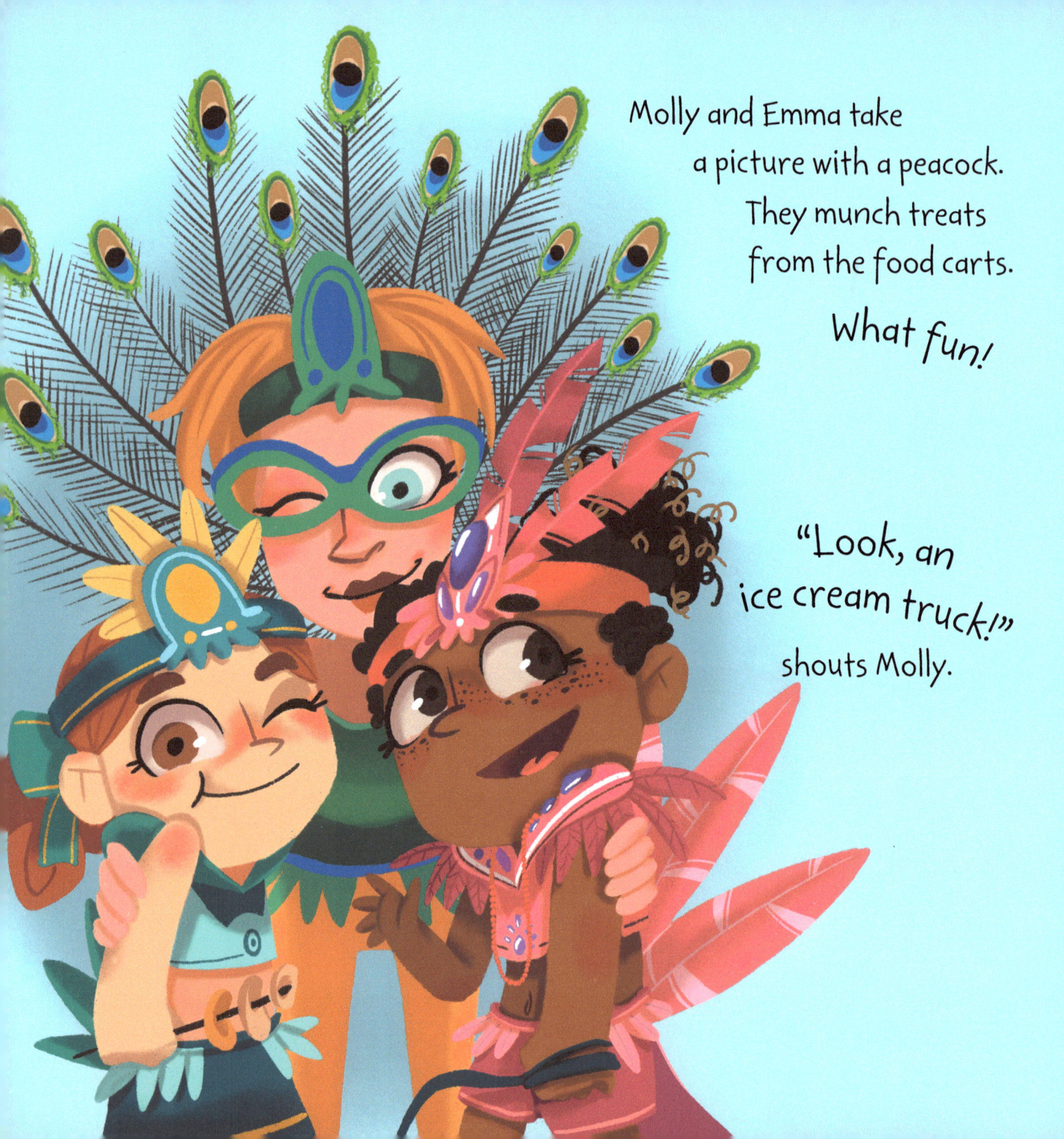

Molly and Emma take a picture with a peacock. They munch treats from the food carts.

What *fun!*

"Look, an ice cream truck!" shouts Molly.

But as she races to the truck, WHACK! A big green dragon bumps into her, almost knocking her down.

"Sorry," shouts the dragon, as he disappears into the crowd.

Molly tries to hold onto her crown, Boomer's leash, and her ice cream cone all at the same time.

"Oh no! I lost another feather!" she squeals.
"Now what? My costume! The prize! How will I win?"

"Don't worry, you still have one feather left," says Emma. "You can still win."

Molly's last feather flops to the ground.

"I won't win now," Molly sobs, as tears and raindrops run down her face and onto her beautiful costume.

Molly wipes the tears from her eyes and looks around.

Feathers and masks are all over the ground. Glitter is running down kids' faces. But everyone is still laughing and dancing!

"Emma," Molly says, "it doesn't matter if my costume is wet and soggy and all my feathers are gone. I can still have fun—even if I don't win the best costume award."

So, Molly blows her whistle ...

and waves her flag ...

and continues to dance.

Molly has the best time ever.

That night, as Papa tucks Molly into bed, he says, "I'm sorry you didn't win the prize.

"That's okay," says Molly. "There's always next year!"

Molly Morningstar is already imagining an even grander costume.

Also Available in the
Molly Morningstar series:

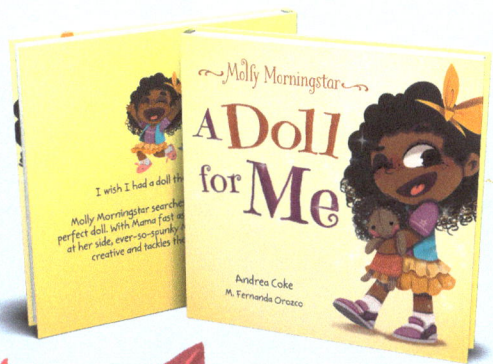

Grab free activity and coloring sheets at **www.abcbooknook.com** or scan here.

Educator by day, children's author by night! Creating engaging children's stories that embrace well-being, diversity, and inclusion is where Andrea Coke's heart lies. After a childhood of inserting herself into other people's experiences, Andrea is thrilled to bring to life books for kids that reflect their own experiences. She is the author of the Molly Morningstar book series.

Proud Canadian mom of four, Andrea is originally from the twin islands of Trinidad and Tobago.

Carnival Girl is the second book in the Molly Morningstar series.

M. Fernanda is an illustrator and graphic designer from Guatemala, based in Spain, that enjoys translating messages, ideas, even worlds into dynamic illustrations.

She has loved books since she was a little girl and was always reading. That's probably the reason why she is always excited to be part of projects involving children's literature and drawings that will give new readers a wonderful experience while reading.

CPSIA information can be obtained
at www.ICGtesting.com
Printed in the USA
LVHW070819050322
712266LV00012B/47